TOP 10

PARENTS KEEP OUT!

Deadly
Animals

A FIREFLY BOOK

Published by Firefly Books Ltd. 2015

First printing

Publisher Cataloging-in-Publication Data (U.S.)

A CIP record for this title is available from the Library of Congress

Library and Archives Canada Cataloguing in Publication

A CIP record for this title is available from Library and Archives Canada

Published in the United States by
Firefly Books (U.S.) Inc.
P.O. Box 1338, Ellicott Station
Buffalo, New York 14205

Published in Canada by
Firefly Books Ltd.
50 Staples Avenue, Unit 1
Richmond Hill, Ontario L4B 0A7

Printed in China

First published in Great Britain in 2015 by Ticktock,
an imprint of Octopus Publishing Group Ltd
Endeavour House
189 Shaftesbury Avenue
London, WC2H 8JY
Commissioning Editor: Anna Bowles
Senior Production Manager: Peter Hunt

TOP 10

PARENTS KEEP OUT!

Deadly Animals

Paul Terry

FIREFLY BOOKS

TOP 10

Deadly Animals

We're about to take you deep inside a world of razor-sharp fangs, toxic stingers and flesh-tearing claws! The natural world is a place full of wonder, and the species we've got lined up for you in these five zones are going to blow your mind. Our planet's skies, oceans, land masses and even Earth's prehistoric past are about to be put under the Team T-10 microscope. Take a deep breath, and let's get deadly...

CONTENTS

ZONE 1
Deadliest of Them All! 8

Most Deadly 10
Biggest Carnivores 12
Most Frightening Jaws 14
Most Bizarre Ways To Kill 16
Amazing Predatory Battles 18
Largest Pack Numbers 20
Most Toxic 22
Biggest Bloodsuckers 24
Biggest Human Parasites 26
Coolest Deadly Animal Movies 28

ZONE 2
Deadliest on Land 30

Biggest Carnivores On Land 32
Scariest Land Predators 34
Fastest Land Predators 36
Largest Big Cats 38
Most Frightening Weapons 40
Endangered Land Predators 42
Biggest Carnivorous Reptiles 44
Longest Snakes 46
Largest Spiders 48
Most Venomous Insects 50

ZONE 3
Deadliest in the Water 52

Biggest Sharks 54
Fastest Aquatic Predators 56
Most Poisonous Fish 58
Most Terrifying Aquatic Monsters 60
Areas With The Most Shark Attacks 62
Biggest River Monsters 64

ZONE 4
Deadliest in the Skies 66

Scariest Carnivorous Birds 68
Fastest Airborne Predators 70
Biggest Eagles 72
Deadliest Flying Insects 74
Flying Freaks 76

ZONE 5
Deadliest Prehistoric Predators 78

Biggest Carnivorous Dinosaurs 80
Widest Prehistoric Wingspans 82
Largest Ocean Beasts 84
Biggest Prehistoric Carnivorous Mammals 86
Weirdest Prehistoric Creatures 88
Most Terrifying Dino Weaponry 90

MEET...
TEAM T-10

Before you dive into this fact-packed adventure, say hello to the super team who are ready to guide you through the amazing info zones.

MAY-TRIX

T-10 FILE

This technology-loving 10-year-old girl is the eldest of Team T-10. May-Trix has hundreds of gadgets and gizmos that she uses to scan her surroundings for exciting data. From analyzing animals' sizes and special abilities, to understanding robotics and space exploration, May-Trix adores it all.

T-10 FILE

There are the *Guardians of the Galaxy*, then there's the Keeper of the Comics... And that's Apollo! This 8-year-old boy is an amazing comic book artist, and knows everything there is to know about superheroes, movies, video games, TV shows and cartoons. He's into sport and outer space, too.

APOLLO

T-10 FILE

When it comes to extreme sports, fast vehicles, video games and slammin' rock music, 9-year-old Shaun is your guy! He doesn't go anywhere without his headphones, and he loves cool buildings (he designs skate parks, too). His cybernetic artificial arm allows him to do gravity-defying skateboard tricks.

SHAUN VERT

T-10 FILE

Quantum is a very special 7-year-old. Her best friend is her cyborg fish Cy-Go, and her quantum-powered goldfish bowl means she can travel through time and space to learn about the past, the future and the furthest reaches of the universe! This pair love to relax with a movie as well.

QUANTUM

ZONE 1
Deadliest of Them All!

Terrifying teeth, lethal venom and giant predators rule these pages....

TOP 10 Most Deadly

Which creatures do you think pose the biggest threat to humans? The results are in and you may be surprised to find there's not a shark in sight.

	CREATURE	HUMAN DEATHS PER YEAR
1	Mosquito	1,000,000
2	Tsetse Fly	300,000
3	Indian Cobra	50,000
4	Buthidae Family of Scorpions	3,250
5	Saltwater Crocodile	1,000+
6	Hippopotamus	500+
7	Elephant	500
8	Cape Buffalo	200+
9	African Lion	150
10	Australian Box Jellyfish	90

SIZE 'EM UP

ELEPHANT
WEIGHT: 7,000 kg (15,000 lb)

AFRICAN LION
WEIGHT: 191 kg (420 lb)

MAN
WEIGHT: 75 kg (165 lb)

HUNGRY HIPPOS!

These herbivores eat 45 kg (100 lb) of grass each day, but they're incredibly aggressive – even crocs keep their distance! They can sprint at 30 km/h (19 mph), so steer clear.

MOSQUITO MADNESS!

Mosquito bites can be deadly because these creatures spread dangerous parasites and viruses through feasting on human and animal blood. What's really crazy? Mosquitoes are unaffected by what they carry!

the **lowdown**...

Indian Cobra

As if this snake wasn't imposing enough to look at, it has hollow fangs that can spray venom at victims who are up to 2 m (6 ft) away. Its bite is so lethal that it can cause a fatal heart attack in just 15 minutes. It is one of four snake species that are responsible for the most bites in India.

KILLER FACT

As soon as they're born, baby Indian Cobras have lethal venom ready to use.

SALTWATER CROCS ARE LIKE THE ULTIMATE SUPER-VILLAIN: SCARILY STRONG, AWESOME ATTACK SKILLS AND THAT EVIL SMILE!

KILLER FACT

This massive meat-eating mammal can grow to 3.35 m (11 ft) tall and has a row of 42 jagged teeth. A Polar Bear has an amazing sense of smell and can detect food nearly 1.6 km (1 mile) away.

the **lowdown**...

Polar Bear

Living to 25 years of age, these endangered animals (approx. 25,000 left) spend a huge amount of their lives in the ocean, which explains why their Latin name is *Ursus maritimus* – meaning "sea bear." They've been recorded performing long-distance swims of 354 km (220 miles)!

TOP 10 Biggest Carnivores

Being a meat-eater doesn't mean you have to be a flesh-ripper, as the number one in this list proves. However, all 10 do have one thing in common: they are amazing examples of biology operating on a HUGE scale.

	TYPE	NAME	HEAVIEST RECORDED (KG)	(LB)
1	Whale	Blue Whale	189,999	418,877
2	Shark	Whale Shark	21,318	47,000
3	Dolphin	Killer Whale	9,979	22,000
4	Seal	Southern Elephant Seal	4,990	11,000
5	Crocodile	Saltwater Crocodile	2,000	4,409
=	Walrus	Pacific Walrus	2,000	4,409
7	Bear	Polar Bear	1,002	2,209
8	Stingray	Giant Freshwater Stingray	600	1,320
9	Big Cat	Siberian Tiger	500	1,102
10	Squid	Colossal Squid	495	1,091

GIANT SHARK

Don't be scared if you swim near a Whale Shark, as they are "filter-feeders." Like Baleen Whales, they use that huge mouth to scoop up loads of tiny fish and plankton. This is where they get the "whale" part of their name from.

SIZE 'EM UP

Let's get the scale of the situation... Look at the size of these beasts!

WOW... THE GIANT FRESHWATER STINGRAY WAS ONLY DISCOVERED IN 2004!

POLAR BEAR

SIBERIAN TIGER

TOP 10 Most Frightening Jaws

If you think going to the dentist is scary, imagine saying, "Open wide" to THESE 10 animals.

	ANIMAL	BITE FORCE PSI
1	Nile Crocodile	5,000
2	Great White Shark	4,000
3	Alligator	2,000
4	Hippopotamus	1,800
5	Gorilla	1,300
6	Hyena	1,100
7	Tiger	1,000
=	Alligator Snapping Turtle	1,000
9	Harpy Eagle	910
10	Bear	750

WHAT'S PSI?
Pounds per square inch is a special method of measuring pressure.

HARPY EAGLE

KILLER FACT

Scientists have calculated the *T. rex* could have had a bite pressure of 5,805 kg (12,800 lb)!

TEAM T-10 REPORT

Jaw-dropping!

We've brought together some terrifying teeth here, but can you think of any other animals with super-scary jaws? What about prehistoric creatures? Or the weirdest mouths in the insect kingdom?

Nile Crocodile

This African beast is a VERY aggressive predator and will eat anything, no matter what it is! Its teeth are designed for gripping, not slicing, and its "death roll" body spin can kill prey in seconds. Once it sinks its teeth in there's no escape!

the lowdown...

SIZE 'EM UP

Check out these tooth size comparisons!

HUMAN
GORILLA
ALLIGATOR
GREAT WHITE SHARK

the **lowdown**...

Assassin Bug

This silent assassin is one of nature's most devious creations. See that long mouth-part? This bug injects toxins into its victim, which melt its insides! Then it's an easy (but disgusting) case of drinking it up. No need for a straw!

VIPERFISH
ACTUAL SIZE!

MY GOLDFISH CY-GO MAY HAVE CYBORG SKILLS, BUT EVEN SHE'S SCARED OF THE VIPERFISH'S LONG FANGS!

TOP 10 Most Bizarre Ways To Kill

Squeamish? Then you'd better look away. Team T-10 is about to list some of the startling, gory and just really WACKY ways that predators catch and kill their prey!

AMAZINGLY, EVEN THOUGH THIS EEL CAN GENERATE 600 VOLTS TO SHOCK ITS PREY, IT DOES NO HARM TO ITSELF!

	ANIMAL	METHOD USED
1	Electric Eel	Electric shock
2	Python	Swallows huge prey alive and whole
3	Crocodile	The death roll
4	Praying Mantis	Female eats male after mating
5	African Rock Python	Crushes and suffocates then eats whole
6	Viperfish	Dislocates jaw to eat
7	Amazonian Tree Ant	Builds traps and dismembers prey
8	Hagfish	Burrows into victim and eats it inside out
9	Assassin Bug	Injects toxin via mouth tube
10	Football Fish	Lit branches on head attract prey

KILLER FACT

Here's Africa's largest snake, the 7 m (23 ft) long Rock Python, swallowing an Impala whole! After eating, the snake may rest for weeks. In this engorged state, it's most vulnerable to attack by other predators.

TOP 10

Amazing Predatory Battles

Possibly the craziest fact in this entire book is that ALL of the battles below really happen in the wild!

SIZE 'EM UP

These razor-clawed mammals are known to fight in the wild, but how do their stats stack up?

PUMA
WEIGHT:
100 kg (220 lb)
HEIGHT (REARING UP):
1.8 m (5.9 ft)

BROWN BEAR
WEIGHT:
635 kg (1,400 lb)
HEIGHT (STANDING):
2.8 m (9.2 ft)

THE STRENGTH OF THE MORAY EEL'S BITE IS OFTEN TOO MUCH FOR AN OCTOPUS TO RECOVER FROM.

the **lowdown...**

Hyena vs. Lion

This battle of the predators happens a lot – these big cats have and always will be enemies in their African home. Fangs and fur fly, and they often try to steal each other's food.

REAL-LIFE BATTLES

1	**Alligator vs. Python**
2	Black Mamba vs. Crowned Hawk-Eagle
3	Moray Eel vs. Octopus
4	Tiger vs. Crocodile
5	Sea Snake vs. Tiger Shark
6	Puma vs. Brown Bear
7	Lion vs. Hyena
8	Wasp vs. Tarantula
9	Lion vs. King Cobra
10	Walrus vs. Polar Bear

KILLER FACT

Beware... Of the four species, Striped and Spotted Hyenas are on record as man-eaters!

TOP 10 Largest Pack Numbers

The T-10 crew obviously think that teamwork is a great thing, so we've assembled a list of the biggest team players in nature.

#	ANIMAL	AVERAGE GROUP SIZE
1	**Army Ant**	**100,000+**
2	Piranha	100+
3	Hyena	UP TO 100
4	Chimpanzee	36
5	Dolphin	15
=	African Lion	15
7	Wolf	10
=	African Wild Dog	10
9	Killer Whale	8
10	Harris Hawk	2–6

KILLER WHALES ARE ALL ABOUT FAMILY. THEY STAY TOGETHER FOR LIFE, AND OFTEN THEIR "POD" HAS FOUR GENERATIONS!

SIZE 'EM UP

Numbers are one thing, but seeing a visual example of these pack hunters really shows the scale of things, especially with Piranhas!

PIRANHAS

CHIMPANZEES

WOLVES

Wolves are very sociable animals. The mom and dad form the core of their pack, with their offspring as the rest.

TEN MILLION YEARS AGO YOU COULD MEET THE MEGAPIRANHA. IT HAD A BITE THREE TIMES STRONGER THAN AN ALLIGATOR'S!

ARMY ANTS REALLY DO HAVE COMIC BOOK-STYLE SUPER-STRENGTH: THEY CAN LIFT 20 TIMES THEIR BODY WEIGHT!

the **lowdown...**

Chimpanzees

Don't ever cross these guys in the wild. Adult males are the most aggressive, and are extremely protective of their territory. Chimpanzees are known to target and kill smaller monkeys too. They live to around 40 years old in the wild.

KILLER **FACT**

Chimps use many different faces and gestures to communicate with each other. When they are preparing to attack, they press their lips together tightly.

21

TOP 10 Most Toxic

Even some of the most beautiful and delicate-looking creatures can hide a fatal venomous trick, especially these toxic 10.

BLUE-RINGED OCTOPUS

There is no anti-venom available for the sting of the Blue-Ringed Octopus, making it one of the deadliest creatures to humans in the ocean.

	ANIMAL	NUMBER OF HUMANS ITS POISON COULD KILL
1	Box Jellyfish	3,600
2	Sea Snake	1,000
3	Inland Taipan Snake	100
4	Blowfish	30
5	Blue-Ringed Octopus	26
6	Fat-Tailed Scorpion	20
=	Marbled Cone Snail	20
8	Stonefish	18
9	Brazilian Wandering Spider	12
10	Golden Poison Dart Frog	10

KILLER FACT

This scorpion's group is classified by the Latin name *Androctonus*, which translates as "man killer."

Beware Frogs!

Scientists are baffled about why the Golden Poison Dart Frog is so toxic. Some think it takes on the poison from the plants and insects it eats or has contact with. There are over 100 different species of Poison Dart Frog, all around 2.5 cm (1 in) long. Look but don't touch!

Fat-Tailed Scorpion

Small but seriously deadly, Fat-Tailed Scorpions are just 10 cm (3.9 in) long. They live mostly in the Middle East and Africa and there are 18 different species. The potent chemicals in their venom makes their victim's insides liquefy once they've been stung. Yuk!

the lowdown...

SIZE 'EM UP

With one figure representing 100 people, here's how potent these creatures' toxic powers are. Keep well clear!

Each icon represents 100 deaths

BOX JELLYFISH

SEA SNAKE

INLAND TAIPAN SNAKE

THE STONEFISH HAS AN AMAZING ABILITY TO BLEND IN PERFECTLY WITH ITS SEABED SURROUNDINGS, HENCE ITS NAME. THE TROUBLE IS, SWIMMERS THEN ACCIDENTALLY STEP ON IT AND GET STUNG.

TOP 10 Biggest Blood Suckers

If you thought vampires were just the stuff of legend, think again. The animal kingdom has some very creepy creatures that love to suck the blood of the living, and in some cases, even the dead!

the lowdown...

Vampire Bat

The Common Vampire Bat, White-winged Vampire Bat and Hairy-legged Vampire Bat all have a wingspan of approx. 18 cm (7 in). They all feed exclusively on a diet of blood, but the Common guys like cows and horses, whereas the other two types prefer the blood of birds. After feasting, they gain an extra 30% of their body weight in blood.

A REAL DRACULA!
The Vampire Bat's saliva stops the host's blood from clotting.

BLOOD-FEEDING CATFISH

Check out this very dark Candirú tale that Team T-10 discovered. Although this tiny fish usually sneaks inside a fish's gills to drink its blood. one swam up into a man's penis while he was peeing in the River Amazon!

Bedbug Biters!

...But did you know there's a great way to stop them sucking your blood you while you sleep? Bedbug detection dogs! It's 100 percent true — some dogs are being trained to seek out the smell Bedbugs give off!

BLOODSUCKER	LENGTH (CM)	(IN)
1 Sea Lamprey	**90**	**35.5**
2 Giant Amazon Leech	45.7	18
3 Candirú	40	16
4 Vampire Bat	18	7
5 Vampire Finch	12	4.7
6 Madrilenial Butterfly	7	2.76
7 Assassin Bug	4	1.6
8 Female Mosquito	1.6	0.6
9 Bedbug	0.5	0.2
10 Flea	0.25	0.09

SEA LAMPREYS ARE SUCKERS THAT HAVE SURVIVED THE PREHISTORIC ERA!

KILLER FACT

The Vampire Finch takes "feeling peckish" to a super-dark place. It jabs its beak into the necks of other birds on its Galápagos Islands home and then sips the blood from the wound!

ASSASSIN BUGS ARE ALSO KNOWN AS KISSING BUGS, AND NEARLY ALL 130 SPECIES DRINK BLOOD.

ASSASSIN BUG
LENGTH: 90 cm (35.5 in)

Biggest Human Parasites

From the bloodsuckers on the previous pages, we now take you into the even DARKER waters... where creatures feast on us!

	CREATURE	LENGTH (METERS)
1	**Pork Tapeworm**	**50**
2	Beef Tapeworm	12
3	Raw Fish Tapeworm	9.14
=	Whale Tapeworm	9.14
5	Roundworm	1
6	Rat Tapeworm	0.6
7	Bertiella Tapeworm	0.13
8	Fasciola Gigantica Flatworm	0.10
=	Cyclophyllidea Tapeworm	0.10
10	Fasciolopsis Buski Fluke	0.075

KILLER FACT

Contaminated meat can contain Pork Tapeworm larvae that become adults in 12 weeks.

ZONE 1: Deadliest of them all!

PORK TAPEWORM

Once Pork Tapeworms are removed from their human hosts, there might still be some surprises to come. These disgusting creatures lay up to 50,000 eggs that can stay in the small intestine for years. Avoid eating pork that's off or undercooked!

YOU MAY BE THINKING THAT THE *FASCIOLOPSIS BUSKI* FLUKE IS LESS REVOLTING BECAUSE OF ITS SMALLER SIZE, BUT HOW DOES "IT LAYS 25,000 EGGS EVERY DAY" GRAB YOU?

SIZE 'EM UP

PORK TAPEWORM THE LENGTH OF **28** MEN!

In a lot of tapeworm infections, the creature is about 3 m (10 ft) long, but in some (very unfortunate) cases, it can grow to an alarming 50 m (164 ft)!

BRAIN DRAIN!

In 2013, Brit Sherry Fuller, volunteering in Madagascar, nearly died from Pork Tapeworms making their way into her brain! It took 2 years for her to fully recover.

SOME TAPEWORMS HAVE LIVED INSIDE THEIR HUMAN HOSTS FOR 25 YEARS... YUK!

the *lowdown*...

Roundworm

It may sound like an alien invasion, but Roundworms are currently using a QUARTER of the world's population as hosts! Infection occurs if you swallow their eggs (found in contaminated water or food): a downside to globetrotting.

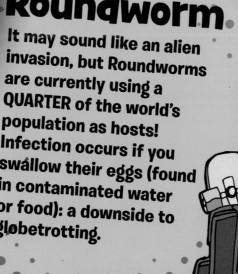

Jurassic Park

The fourth instalment is *Jurassic World* (2015), but director Steven Spielberg's *Jurassic Park* (1993) is where it all began. The roar accompanying the full-scale puppet and CGI (computer-generated imagery) of *T. rex* was a combination of elephant, alligator, tiger, penguin and dog sounds.

MARVEL COMICS MAY HAVE FEATURED THE CHITAURI BEFORE, BUT THE LEVIATHANS WERE CREATED SPECIALLY FOR THE AVENGERS MOVIE!

KILLER FACT

Godzilla (2014) was released 60 years after the original movie, and harks back to its plot and 'Zilla's origins. If one computer had been tasked to finish all 960 visual effects, it would've taken 450 years!

THE HUNGER GAMES: CATCHING FIRE

That terrifying monkey-mutt attack on Katniss featured some amazing CGI of the crazed creatures. They were created by Weta, who crafted the effects for the likes of *Dawn Of The Planet Of The Apes* and *The Lord Of The Rings* movies.

ZONE 1: Deadliest of them all!

TOP 10

Coolest Deadly Animal Movies

Team T-10 loves monster movies more than any other kind, so coming up with a list for you was a walk in the park.

	MOVIE	YEAR RELEASED	MOST DEADLY BEAST(S)
1	Godzilla	2014	M.U.T.O.s, Godzilla
2	How To Train Your Dragon	2010	Red Death Dragon
3	The Avengers	2012	Chitauri Leviathans
4	The Lord Of The Rings: The Fellowship Of The Ring	2001	Balrog, Cave Troll
5	Jurassic Park	1993	Velociraptors, *T. rex*
6	The Hobbit: The Desolation Of Smaug	2013	Smaug
7	Thor: The Dark World	2013	Jötunheim Frost Monster
8	The Hunger Games: Catching Fire	2013	Crazed monkeys
9	Pacific Rim	2013	Kaiju
10	Pirates Of The Caribbean: Dead Man's Chest	2006	Kraken

BOX OFFICE

Each icon represents over $48 million

THE AVENGERS
$1,473,669,146

JURASSIC PARK
$998,707,630

THE RED DEATH DRAGON WAS EVIL AND BRUTAL, BUT ALSO VERY SMART. IT GOT ALL OF THE OTHER DRAGONS TO GATHER FOOD FOR IT!

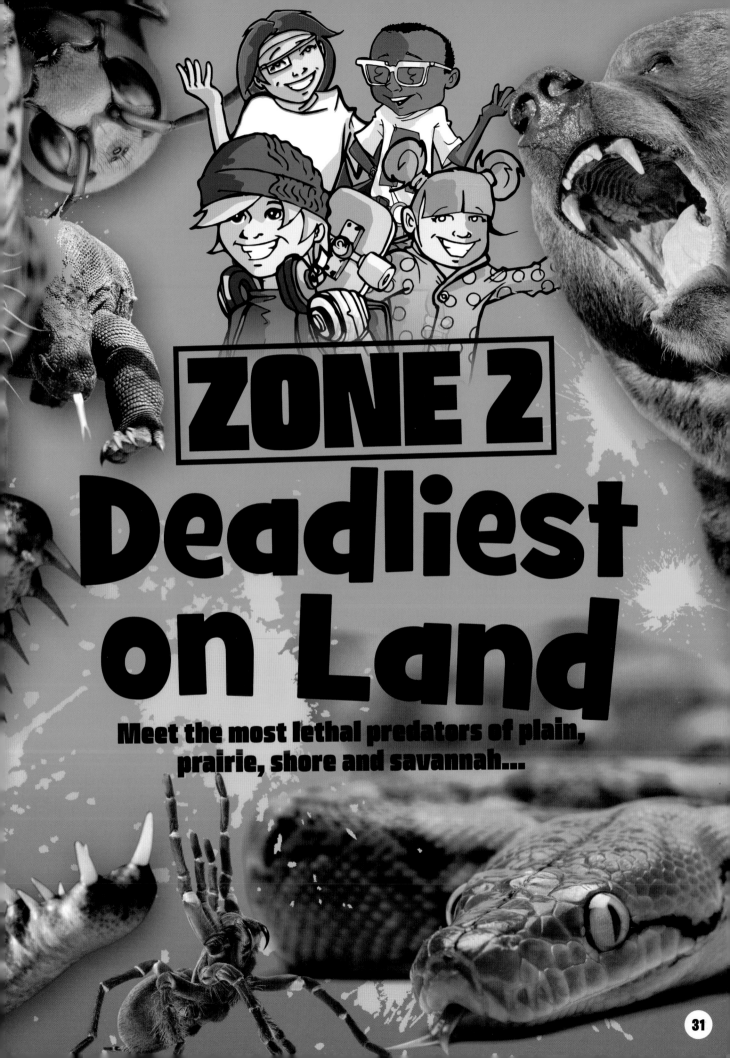

ZONE 2
Deadliest on Land

Meet the most lethal predators of plain, prairie, shore and savannah...

KILLER FACT

Being an island species, the Kodiak bear has been genetically isolated for around 12,000 years (since the last ice age on Earth). They mainly eat fish.

the lowdown...

Kodiak Brown Bear

Kodiak Brown Bears get their name from their home, the Kodiak Archipelago, a group of islands in south-western Alaska. They are one of the largest bears in the world but Kodiak Brown Bears are actually quite shy and generally steer clear of humans on the island.

TOP 10 Biggest Carnivores On Land

We've already taken a look at the largest meat-eaters on the planet. Here we focus on the land heavyweights!

	TYPE	WEIGHT (KG)	(LB)
1	Southern Elephant Seal	4,989	11,000
2	Saltwater Crocodile	2,000	4,409
3	Pacific Walrus	2,000	4,409
4	Black Caiman	1,310	2,900
5	Polar Bear	1,002	2,209
6	Gharial	977	2,150
7	Kodiak Brown Bear	967	2,132
8	Grizzly Bear	680	1,499
9	Brown Bear	635	1,400
10	Siberian Tiger	500	1,102

BIG SEAL!

Fancy meeting a Southern Elephant Seal? At up to 6.85 m (22.5 ft) long, we wouldn't recommend asking one for directions to the best fishing spots...

SOUTHERN ELEPHANT SEAL

POLAR vs. KODIAK

On average, these two bears are virtually the same size. The biggest Kodiak Brown Bear recorded was 966.15 kg (2,130 lb), so the largest Polar Bear beats it by 36 kg (79 lb).

POLAR BEAR

KODIAK BEAR

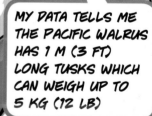

MY DATA TELLS ME THE PACIFIC WALRUS HAS 1 M (3 FT) LONG TUSKS WHICH CAN WEIGH UP TO 5 KG (12 LB)

TOP 10 Scariest Land Predators

This list has got it all: lethal venoms, slashing claws, powerful jaws and crushing, suffocating skills...

ANIMAL

1	**Komodo Dragon**
2	**Saltwater Crocodile**
3	**Tiger**
4	**Indian Cobra**
5	**Huntsman Spider**
6	**Grizzly Bear**
7	**Hyena**
8	**Lion**
9	**Black Mamba**
10	**Anaconda**

DRAGON FEAST
Komodos can get by on merely 10-12 big meals a year.

Black Mamba
The Black Mamba is the speediest snake, reaching 20 km/h (12 mph)! Its name refers to its blue-black mouth, which contains the fastest-acting venom of all snakes.

ANACONDAS GROW TO 7.6 M (25 FT) LONG! THAT'S THE LENGTH OF TWO FAMILY CARS PUT END TO END!

the lowdown...

Komodo Dragon

These mythical-looking beasts were only discovered about 100 years ago, but they've been on Earth for millions of years and are genuinely prehistoric lizards. They will attack anything, including humans, and their flexible jaws mean they can swallow large prey whole.

HUNTSMAN SPIDER

The Huntsman is the biggest spider of them all at 30 cm (11.8 in) across. It lives for about 2 years and can lay 200 eggs at a time. Its bite is venomous, but not fatal to humans.

TOP 10 Fastest Land Predators

You can be a mammal, reptile or insect to make this list. You've just got to be FAST!

A CHEETAH CAN ACCELERATE FOUR TIMES FASTER THAN A HUMAN AND CAN SLOW DOWN BY 14 KM/H (8.7 MPH) IN JUST ONE STRIDE. SWEEEET!

	ANIMAL	SPEED (KM/H)	(MPH)
1	Cheetah	113	70.2
2	Lion	80	49.7
3	African Wild Dog	72	44.7
4	Coyote	69	42.9
5	Tiger	64	40
6	Hyena	60	37
7	Bearded Dragon	40	25
8	Six-Lined Racerunner	32	20
9	Black Mamba	23	14
10	Tiger Beetle	6.8	4.2

COYOTE

You may know these animals as American Jackals. Although they live in large groups, similar to wolf packs, Coyotes tend to hunt in pairs.

36

SIZE 'EM UP

To get a sense of scale, here's how these two racing reptiles compare to one another...

BEARDED DRAGON
LENGTH: 30.5 to 61 cm (12 to 24 in)

SIX-LINED RACERUNNER
LENGTH: 5.5 to 7.5 cm (2.1 to 2.9 in)

KILLER FACT

An adult Bearded Dragon eats mostly vegetation and fruit, but it snacks on insects, too.

the lowdown...

Cheetah

The cheetah's semi-retractable claws help with grabbing prey. Its extinct relation was the Giant Cheetah – twice its size at 117.9 kg (260 lb). The roller coaster Cheetah Hunt at Busch Gardens in Florida travels at 97 km/h (60 mph), which still isn't as fast as a real cheetah.

Jaguar

the lowdown...

Unlike most domesticated cats, Jaguars really enjoy swimming. Lions always live in a pride, (meaning "family"), but Jaguars prefer to live and hunt alone. Their incredibly powerful jaws can crack open turtle shells!

TOP 10 Largest Big Cats

They don't get their name "big cat" for nothing. These massive guys pack a serious paw-powered punch!

	BIG CAT	WEIGHT (KG)	(LB)
1	Tiger	420	925.9
2	Lion	270	595.2
3	Jaguar	140	308.6
4	Cougar	120	264.5
5	Snow Leopard	73	160.9
6	Leopard	64	141.1
7	Cheetah	55	121.2
8	Lynx	35	77.2
9	Clouded Leopard	25	55.1
10	Caracal	20	44.1

SIZE 'EM UP

We've looked at their weight, but let's see how these big cats compare in length...

TIGER
LENGTH:
3.2 m (10.5 ft)

JAGUAR
LENGTH:
1.6 m (5.2 ft)

LYNX
LENGTH:
1 m (3.3 ft)

KILLER FACT

Only male lions have this amazing mane. No other species of big cats have anything similar. The darker the shades of the mane, the healthier the lion is.

LIONS ROCK, BUT MY FAVE, NIMRAVIDAE (A SABER-TOOTHED CAT), LIVED OVER 40 MILLION YEARS AGO!

TOP 10 Most Frightening Weapons

Nature has outfitted all kinds of creatures with some amazing weaponry. Whether it's for defence or hunting, here are 10 that we think deserve a place on our list.

	ANIMAL	WEAPON(S)
1	Polar Bear	5.1 cm (2 in) long claws
2	Caribou	135 cm (53 in) long antlers
3	Stag Beetle	Flying horned beetle with huge jaws
4	Wolverine	Razor-sharp curled claws
5	Komodo Dragon	Strong claws help it climb trees and slash prey
6	Wildebeest	80 cm (32 in) curved horns for fighting
7	Tiger	10 cm (4 in) long claws
8	Saltwater Crocodile	Powerful claws are as tough as fiberglass
9	Grizzly Bear	5.1 cm (2 in) long claws
10	Rhinoceros Beetle	One horn is 60% the length of its whole body

RHINOCEROS BEETLE
LENGTH: 15 CM (6 in)

STAG BEETLE
LENGTH: 3.5 cm to 7.5 cm (1.4 to 3 in)

KILLER **FACT**

There are over 300 different species of Rhinoceros Beetle, and in some Asian countries they are very popular pets!

WOLVERINE

The Marvel Comics' character Wolverine is named after this stocky, aggressive, 25 kg (55 lb) mammal. Although the size of an average dog, the Wolverine is more like a compact, razor-clawed mini-bear.

Horns

Horns are largely made of keratin (the same substance as your fingernails). Animals use them for defence, to guard their territory and to decide who is the dominant male during mating season.

AT 250 KG (551.1 LB), THE WILDEBEEST IS A VERY POWERFUL FOUR-LEGGED VEGETARIAN!

WITH 15 CM (8 IN) LONG CLAWS AND STANDING OVER 3 M (10 FT) HIGH, IT'S NO WONDER THE GRIZZLY BEAR IS A PREDATOR WE SHOULD BE WARY OF.

the lowdown...

Wildebeest

The Wildebeest is actually a kind of antelope, sometimes called a Gnu. Some kinds migrate, and during this hazardous journey their 80 km/h (50 mph) running speed helps them evade predators like crocodiles, lions and hyenas.

POLAR BEAR CLAW

ACTUAL SIZE!

KILLER FACT

Snow Leopards will even hunt Himalayan Tahr – massive horned goats!

ID TELEPORT AWAY FROM THOSE JAWS. THEY BITE PREY ON THE NECK TO TAKE THEM DOWN!

TOP 10 Endangered Land Predators

The deadliest life form on this planet? Sadly, it's us. Our actions have led to these formidable predators being endangered, and now they need our help.

Sumatran Orangutan

These primates are found on the Indonesian island of Sumatra. Along with their Bornean Orangutan relations, they're critically endangered. You can help save them: www.orangutans-sos.org

	ANIMAL	EST. NUMBER REMAINING
1	Panda	1,600
2	Greater One-Horned Rhino	3,000
3	Tiger	3,200
4	Black Rhino	4,848
5	Snow Leopard	6,590
6	Nigeria-Cameroon Chimpanzee	6,500
7	Sumatran Orangutan	7,300
8	Clouded Leopard	10,000
9	Southern White Rhino	20,170
10	Polar Bear	25,000

the lowdown...

Snow Leopard

This magnificent beast is sadly endangered, but you can help – check out http://gifts.worldwildlife.org/gift-center/gifts/Species-Adoptions/Snow-Leopard.aspx. Although it can deal with snow very easily, it spends a lot of time on steep, rocky terrain too. Weird fact: it can't roar, but instead, makes plenty of growling and hissing sounds.

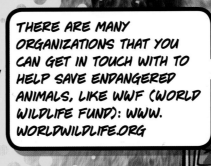

THERE ARE MANY ORGANIZATIONS THAT YOU CAN GET IN TOUCH WITH TO HELP SAVE ENDANGERED ANIMALS, LIKE WWF (WORLD WILDLIFE FUND): WWW.WORLDWILDLIFE.ORG

TOP 10 Biggest Carnivorous Reptiles

The reptile kingdom is full of survivors from the prehistoric age and scaly, powerful predators. To give this list the most variety, we've selected the 10 largest from the different reptile families.

	REPTILE NAME	REPTILE FAMILY	MAXIMUM RECORDED MASS (KG)	(LB)
1	Saltwater Crocodile	Crocodylidae	2,000	4,400
2	Black Caiman	Alligatoridae	1,130	2,900
3	Gharial	Gavialidae	977	2,150
4	Leatherback Sea Turtle	Dermochelyidae	932	2,050
5	Green Anaconda	Boidae	250	550
6	Komodo Dragon	Varanidae	166	370
7	Reticulated Python	Pythonidae	158	350
8	Gaboon Viper	Viperidae	20	44
9	King Cobra	Elapidae	12.7	28
10	Black Rat Snake	Colubridae	2.2	4.9

KILLER FACT

It's not just the mass of the Saltwater Crocodile that makes it so very impressive. How does a length of up to 7.1 m (23 ft) grab you? And its teeth? The longest grow to 9 cm (3.5 in)!

TEAM T-10 REPORT

"Cold" killers!

Rather than using the term "cold-blooded," a better way of describing reptiles' way of maintaining their optimum body temperature is thermoregulation (e.g., moving into sunlight to warm up, etc.).

Gavialidae

Gavialids, like the Gharial, don't have the powerhouse jaws that their reptilian relations do. They have a strikingly long and narrow snout instead, which is perfect for helping them hunt fish. They also enjoy eating amphibians, small crustaceans and insects. Plus, you'll be pleased to know, these crocs do not attack humans!

GHARIAL
LENGTH: 300 to 500 cm
(118 to 197 in)

SALTWATER CROCODILE
LENGTH: 430 to 520 cm
(169 to 205 in)

TOP 10 Longest Snakes

When the shortest snake on this top 10 list is still a 2.44 m (8 ft) long beast, it's a sign that these magnificent creatures grow to sizes that you'd think were reserved only for fictional freaks in movies.

	SNAKE	LONGEST FOUND (M)	(FT)
1	Reticulated Python	14.94	49
2	Green Anaconda	11.28	37
3	Scrub Python	7.92	26
4	African Rock Python	6.1	20
5	King Cobra	5.64	18.5
6	Boa Constrictor	3.96	13
7	Bushmaster	3.05	10
8	Indian Python	2.99	9.8
9	Diamondback Rattlesnake	2.74	8.9
10	Western Rat Snake	2.44	8

A YOUNG BOA CONSTRICTOR CAN CLIMB INTO TREES AND SHRUBS TO FORAGE FOR FOOD.

KILLER FACT

Green Anacondas have no problem attacking and eating adult deer!

THE KING COBRA'S GENERIC NAME "OPHIOPHAGUS" MEANS "SNAKE-EATER" AS ITS DIET CONSISTS MOSTLY OF OTHER SNAKES! IT EATS RATSNAKES, SMALL PYTHONS AND EVEN OTHER VENOMOUS SNAKES.

SIZE 'EM UP

To put their lengths into perspective, here's how they size up in terms of the height of an average human...

RETICULATED PYTHON	GREEN ANACONDA	SCRUB PYTHON	AFRICAN ROCK PYTHON

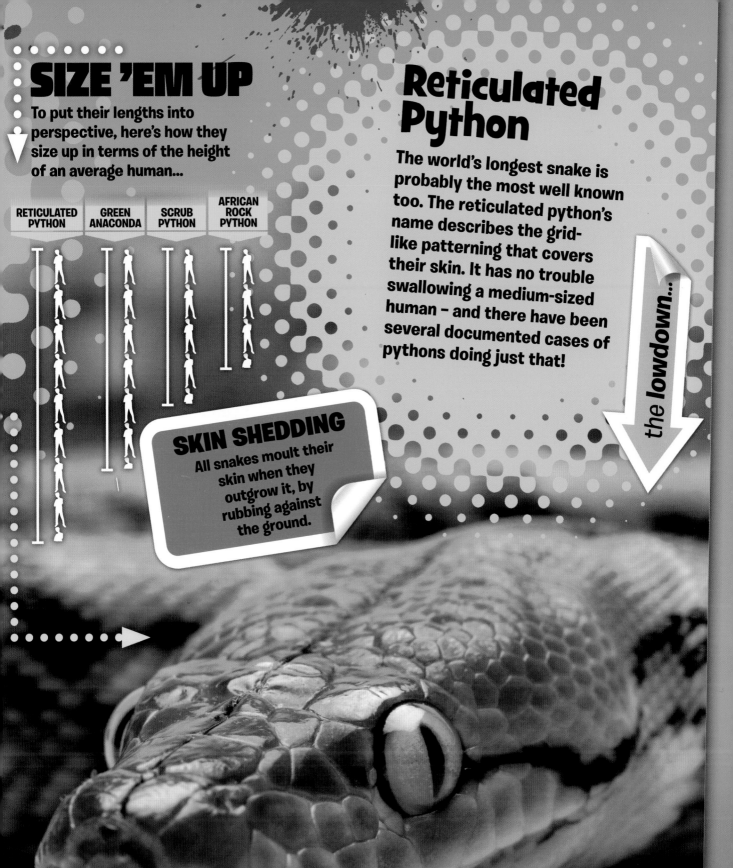

Reticulated Python

The world's longest snake is probably the most well known too. The reticulated python's name describes the grid-like patterning that covers their skin. It has no trouble swallowing a medium-sized human – and there have been several documented cases of pythons doing just that!

the lowdown...

SKIN SHEDDING

All snakes moult their skin when they outgrow it, by rubbing against the ground.

HUNTSMAN
LENGTH: 30 cm (11.8 in)

HYSTEROCRATES
SPELLENBERGI
LENGTH: 17.8 cm (7 in)

COMMON HOUSE SPIDER
LENGTH: 1 cm (0.4 in)

THERE ARE OVER
40,000 SPECIES
OF SPIDER ALIVE IN
THE WORLD TODAY!

KILLER FACT

The protein-based thread that spiders spin for their webs and to protect their eggs is jaw-droppingly strong. It's half as strong as Kevlar, a fiber used for military-grade body armor!

ZONE 2: Deadliest on land

TOP 10 Largest Spiders

What's the largest spider you've ever seen in your house or in a garden? If it put you on edge, make sure you don't read the following measurements without a friend nearby, as you'll find the sizes horrific!

	SPIDER	LEG SPAN (CM)	LEG SPAN (IN)
1	Huntsman	30	11.8
2	Brazilian Salmon Pink	27	10.6
3	Goliath Bird-Eater	25.4	10
4	Wolf Spider	25.4	10
5	Purple Bloom Bird-Eating Spider	23	9
6	Hercules	20.3	8
7	Hysterocrates spellenbergi	17.8	7
8	Brazilian Wandering Spider	15	5.9
9	Cerbalus aravensis	15	5.9
10	Tegenaria parietina	14	5.5

Spider-Sense

The roots of Spider-Man's "spidey sense" come from real-life spiders' "slit sensilla." This amazing organ gives them the ability to sense unbelievably small pressures on their body, like an insect moving (and the air it moves).

YOU'D THINK THAT SPIDERS WOULDN'T LIVE THAT LONG, BUT THE TARANTULA FAMILY CAN LIVE UP TO 25 YEARS!

the lowdown...

Goliath Bird-Eater

This nocturnal spider loves rainforests, swampland and burrows. Its name is misleading as it doesn't often eat birds, preferring insects, snakes, lizards, amphibians and even rodents.

FANG-TASTIC!

Those two big fangs on the Goliath Bird-Eater? They grow up to 4 cm (1.57 in) long!

TOP 10 Most Venomous Insects

They may be small, but never underestimate the strength and impact of insects! Take these creatures, for example. Their venomous powers are as deadly as they come.

	INSECT	LD50 VALUE* (LETHAL DOSE VALUE) MG PER KG OF BODY WEIGHT
1	Yellow Harvester Ant	0.12
2	Assassin Caterpillar	0.19
3	Red Harvester Ant	0.66
4	Asian Giant Hornet	1.6
5	Paper Wasp	2.4
6	Western Honey Bee	2.8
7	Yellow Jacket	3.5
8	Africanized Honey Bee	7.1
9	Fire Ant	8
10	Bag-Shelter Processionary Caterpillar	11.2

*The lower the value, the more venomous the animal

SPIKY!
The Assassin Caterpillar is covered in hundreds of needles that it uses to inject its victims with venom.

FIRE ANT
Bites from these ants can be fatal to humans if not treated properly!

KILLER **FACT**
The Yellow Jacket is a very aggressive insect. Once it has chosen a target it will often keep on stinging the animal until it runs away.

PAPER WASPS BUILD THEIR NESTS FROM WOOD FIBERS AND PLANT STEMS. THEY MIX THESE MATERIALS WITH THEIR SALIVA TO MAKE THE NEST WATER-RESISTANT. NICE!

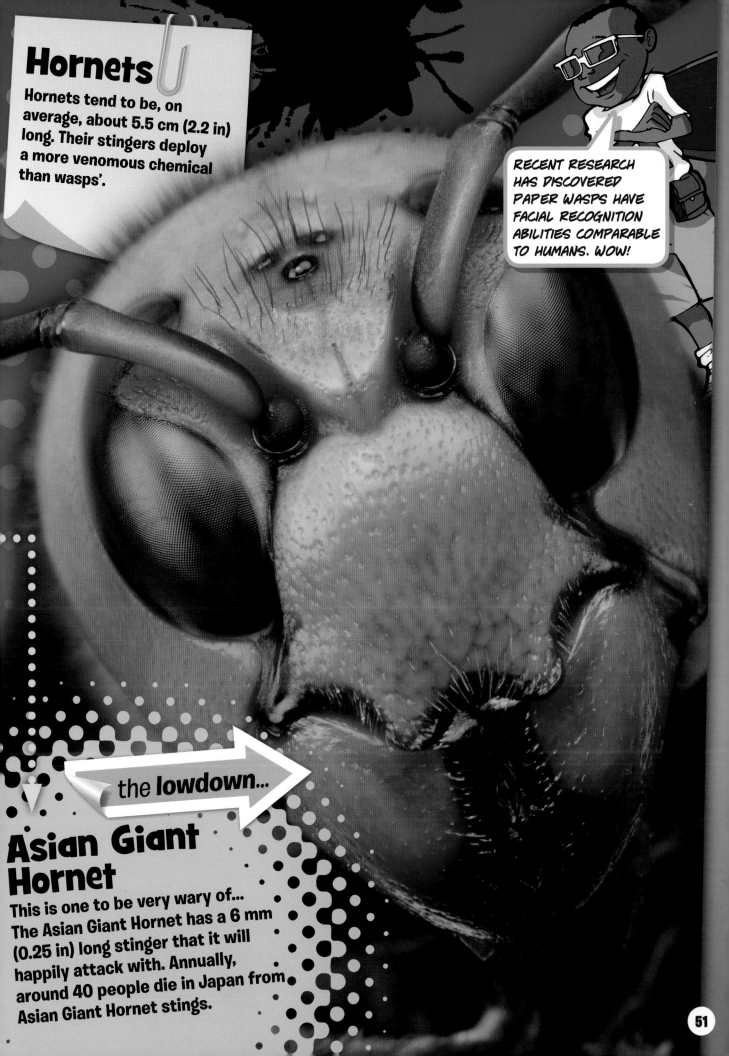

Hornets

Hornets tend to be, on average, about 5.5 cm (2.2 in) long. Their stingers deploy a more venomous chemical than wasps'.

RECENT RESEARCH HAS DISCOVERED PAPER WASPS HAVE FACIAL RECOGNITION ABILITIES COMPARABLE TO HUMANS. WOW!

the **lowdown**...

Asian Giant Hornet

This is one to be very wary of... The Asian Giant Hornet has a 6 mm (0.25 in) long stinger that it will happily attack with. Annually, around 40 people die in Japan from Asian Giant Hornet stings.

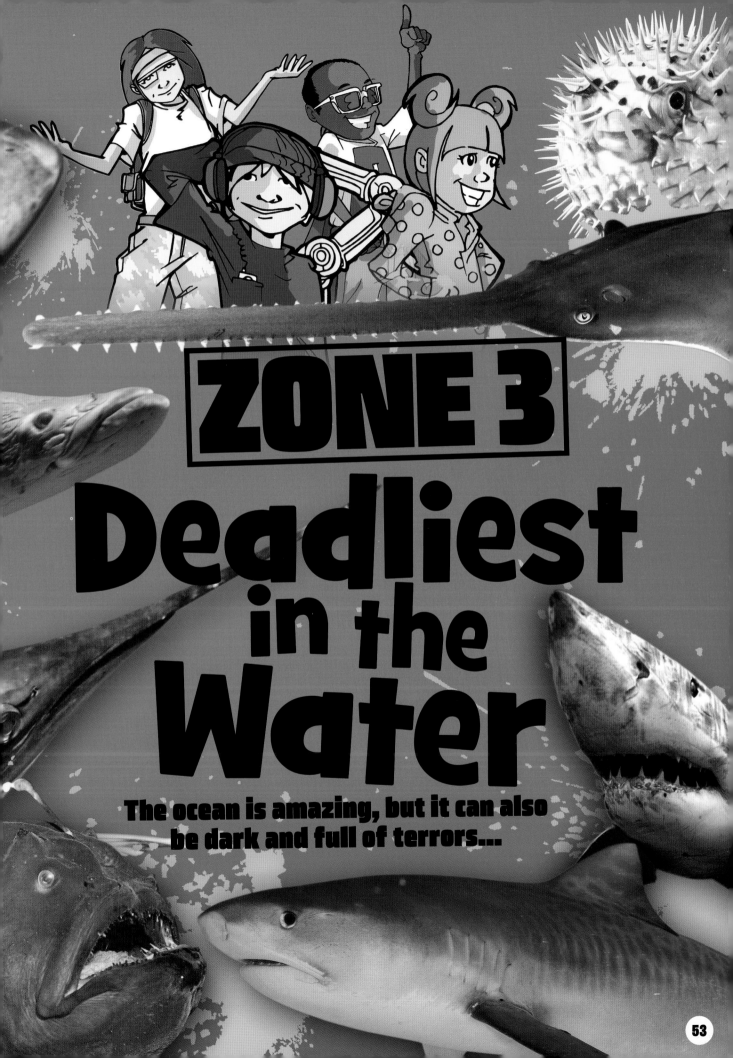

ZONE 3

Deadliest in the Water

The ocean is amazing, but it can also be dark and full of terrors...

TOP 10 Biggest Sharks

It's time to talk about one of Team T-10's fave subjects... Sharks! These finned beasts are some of the most awe-inspiring creatures in the sea, and these are the largest species gliding through our oceans...

	TYPE	LENGTH (M)	(FT)
1	Whale Shark	12.7	41.7
2	Basking Shark	12.3	40.4
3	Great White Shark	8	26.2
4	Tiger Shark	7.4	24.3
=	Pacific Sleeper Shark	7.4	24.3
6	Greenland Shark	6.4	21
7	Great Hammerhead Shark	6.1	20
8	Thresher Shark	6	19.7
9	Bluntnose Sixgill Shark	4.8	15.7
10	Bigeye Thresher Shark	4.6	15.1

MY SCANNER SHOWS THE WHALE SHARK CAN WEIGH 2,1319 KG (47,000 LB)!

the lowdown...

KILLER FACT

Although labelled a "man-eater," shark attacks on humans are often a case of mistaken identity, as on the surface we resemble a seal – many sharks' fave food!

Great White

With a mass of up to 1,208 kg (2,663 lb), this iconic fish is arguably the most famous shark of all. Scientists are mystified by much of the Great White's behavior and life cycle, and this endangered animal needs our help and protection: as few as 1,500 may be left in the world.

EASY TIGER!

This species obviously gets its name from those stripes, but did you know that it's famous for eating pretty much anything? A Tiger Shark loves to chomp on fish, seabirds, crustaceans, smaller sharks and even bits of junk! Some Hawaiians consider it to be a sacred and spiritual animal.

ONE OF ONLY THREE PLANKTON-EATING SHARKS, A BASKING SHARK IS A FILTER-FEEDER, MEANING IT "SIEVES" FOOD OUT OF THE WATER.

BASKING
LENGTH: 12.3 m (41.7 ft)

GREAT WHITE
LENGTH: 8 m (26.2 ft)

TOP 10 Fastest Aquatic Predators

Remember: being a predator doesn't mean you have to hunt BIG prey... All of these ocean dwellers eat other living organisms, and are the speediest ones to sneer at a life of vegetarianism!

	FISH	SPEED (KM/H)	(MPH)
1	Black Marlin	128.75	80
2	Sailfish	110	68.3
3	Mako Shark	95	59
4	Wahoo	78	48.5
5	Bluefin Tuna	70	43.5
6	Great Blue Shark	69	42.9
7	Bonefish	64	39.8
=	Swordfish	64	39.8
9	Great White Shark	56.3	35
10	Killer Whale	56	34.8

SURFERS USUALLY GET UP TO SPEEDS OF AROUND 24.1 KM/H (15 MPH), SO NEXT TIME YOU'RE EATING A TUNA SANDWICH, THINK ABOUT HOW AMAZINGLY FAST THAT FISH CAN GO!

NORMAL GOLDFISH CAN SWIM AT 1.38 KM/H (0.86 MPH), BUT MY CY-GO CAN GO 10 TIMES THAT!

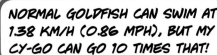
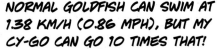

Sailfish

These striking fish grow VERY quickly, getting to 1.5 m (5 ft) long in their first year! Their amazing sail comes in handy when they're hunting for fish to eat: raising the sail spooks smaller fish so they can be herded into a place where picking them off for dinner is a lot easier. Smart fish!

the lowdown...

KILLER FACT

Wahoo have razor-sharp teeth and can grow to 83 kg (183 lb).

DID YOU KNOW?

Sailfish can weigh a massive 90.7 kg (200 lb).

SIZE 'EM UP

Ever wondered how YOU would size up compared to these fish? Wonder no more...

MAKO SHARK

AVG. HEIGHT OF A MAN

BLACK MARLIN

SAILFISH

TOP 10 Most Poisonous Fish

Some species' poisonous qualities pose problems for creatures that try to eat them, or they might use venom to defend themselves...

FISH

1	**Pufferfish**
2	**Stonefish**
3	**Lionfish**
4	**Stingray**
5	**Striped Eel Catfish**
6	**Spotted Trunkfish**
7	**Scorpionfish**
8	**Ghost Shark**
9	**Common Stargazer**
10	**Dogfish Shark**

the lowdown...

Lionfish

This spiny fellow has a clever technique when it attacks prey – it blows a jet of water at its target to disorientate them before it strikes! Other fish, including sharks, eat Lionfish, but scientists do not yet know if the venom affects them.

SIZE 'EM UP

Here's the chart's number four and five next to one another to show their sizes...

STINGRAY
LENGTH: 2 m (6.5 ft)

STRIPED EEL CATFISH
LENGTH: 0.3 m (1 ft)

TEAM T-10 REPORT

Deep trouble

Diving to depths of 200 m (656.2 feet), the Ghost Shark is also called the Elephant Shark because of its trunk-like nose. It uses a venomous spine hidden inside its dorsal fin for defence. Spooky!

PUFFERFISH

One of the most poisonous animals on the planet, yet Pufferfish is a delicacy to eat! It takes years to learn how to serve it safely. Team T-10 will stick to looking at pictures of it!

KILLER FACT

The venom in the Lionfish's fin spikes can be fatal to humans if not treated in time.

TOP 10 Most Terrifying Aquatic Monsters

If you came face-to-face with any of these creatures from the deep, the look of them alone would be enough to give you nightmares! We feel sorry for the little fish who have to swim near them every night...

	CREATURE	APPEARANCE
1	Colossal Squid	Near 15.2 m (50 ft) long; real-life tentacled beast
2	Goliath Tigerfish	68+ kg (150+ lb) fish with huge, croc-like teeth
3	Frilled Shark	Snake-like creature 2 m (6.6 ft) long
4	Anglerfish	Glowing "rod" above the face lures prey into its jaws
5	Goblin Shark	Long horn above mouth of hooked teeth that stick out
6	Sloane's Viperfish	Only 0.3 m (1 ft) long, but has terrifying, vampire-like fangs
7	Pacu	A stocky fish with human-like teeth
8	Sarcastic Fringehead	Splits its face open widthways when it attacks
9	Common Stargazer	Nightmarish face that stares upwards
10	Giant Oarfish	6 m (20 ft) long monster that looks like a sea serpent

DID YOU KNOW GIANT OARFISH ARE THE WORLD'S LONGEST BONY FISH? THE BIGGEST RECORDED GIANT OARFISH WEIGHED IN AT 272 KG (600 LB)!

Pacu

This 1 m (3.3 ft) long South American fish has the creepiest teeth. They may not be razor-sharp, but they make Team T-10 shudder because they look like... HUMAN teeth!

Anglerfish

DID YOU KNOW?
Goblin Sharks can live in shallow waters of 100 m (330 ft) depth.

the lowdown...

The Anglerfish's lure has a bright light. This amazing skill is called "bioluminescence" – the ability to generate light biologically by creating a chemical reaction within the body. It can be used for communication, defence against predators or, in the Anglerfish's case, a sneaky way to grab its dinner.

KILLER FACT

The Museum of New Zealand Te Papa Tongarewa has a preserved Colossal Squid measuring a massive 4.2 m (14 ft) long and weighing 495 kg (1,091 lb).

COLOSSAL SQUID

TOP 10 Areas With The Most Shark Attacks

We love to explore and play in the sea, which can sometimes have dire consequences because we are putting ourselves into a world where we are not the top of the food chain... We potentially ARE food...

	LOCATION	FATAL ATTACKS	TOTAL ATTACKS (reported since 1580)
1	USA*	36	1055
2	Australia	202	704
3	Africa	93	339
4	Asia	48	129
5	Hawaii	10	129
6	Pacific Islands/Oceania*	49	126
7	South America	26	117
8	Antilles and Bahamas	16	70
9	Mexico and Central America	27	57
10	Europe	27	49

*Excludes Hawaii

Australia

Although Australia has the most fatal shark attacks, the number is still low when you consider fewer than one in every 3 million scuba dives in Western Australia ends with a fatal attack.

EUROPEAN HOLIDAYS

The last fatal shark attack in Europe was in 1989. Although the number of total attacks is the lowest here, 55 percent of them were fatal, which is the highest ratio of deaths to attacks across all the countries listed above.

BLUE SHARK
LENGTH: 3.8 m (12 ft)

the lowdown...

Hawaii

The Hawaiian word for shark is "mano," and some people believe sharks are their ancestors returning in a new form to protect them and their home. With surfing so popular in Hawaii, and over 40 species of sharks in its waters, attacks do occur.

KILLER FACT

Cape Town, South Africa is famous for its shark "attacks" but 25 percent of them are superficial, accidental ones by fish-eating Sand Tiger Sharks and Nurse Sharks.

IF YOU'RE SURFING AND YOU SEE A SHARK WHILE SWIMMING, HEAD TO SHORE AS FAST AS YOU CAN BUT WITH SLOW, LONG STROKES. BIG, PANICKED SPLASHING ATTRACTS SHARKS.

TOP 10 Biggest River Monsters

Only the brave will dare to delve down to the depths of the riverbed with these massive creatures lurking in the deep...

	ANIMAL	LOCATION
1	Giant Freshwater Stingray	Thailand
2	Arapaima	Brazilian Amazon
3	Bull Shark	Australia
4	Wels Catfish	Germany
5	Goonch	India
6	Goliath Tigerfish	Rep. of the Congo, Central Africa
7	Tarpon	Nicaragua
8	Freshwater Sawfish	Australia
9	Wolffish	Rep. of Suriname
10	Longfin Eel	New Zealand

TEAM T-10 REPORT

Giant Freshwater Stingray

This species grows up to 1.9 m (6.3 ft) across and can reach 600 kg (1,300 lb). Its stinger alone can be 38 cm (15 in) long! The International Union for Conservation of Nature has assessed the Giant Freshwater Stingray as endangered.

GOONCH

AVG. HEIGHT OF A MAN

the lowdown...

Freshwater Sawfish

That scary nose area is edged with spikes that make it look like a chainsaw. This is very useful for swiping from side to side on the riverbed to pick up food, and it also makes a great defensive weapon. If prey moves past, that face-saw can also be used to jab them before they are chomped.

Arapaima

Reaching 4.6 m (15 ft) long, this ancient, air-breathing fish is famous for leaping out of the water. Fishermen who have been in its way have been known to suffer tremendous impact injuries – this fish is like a missile!

KILLER FACT

3,000 different species of fish live in the Amazon River!

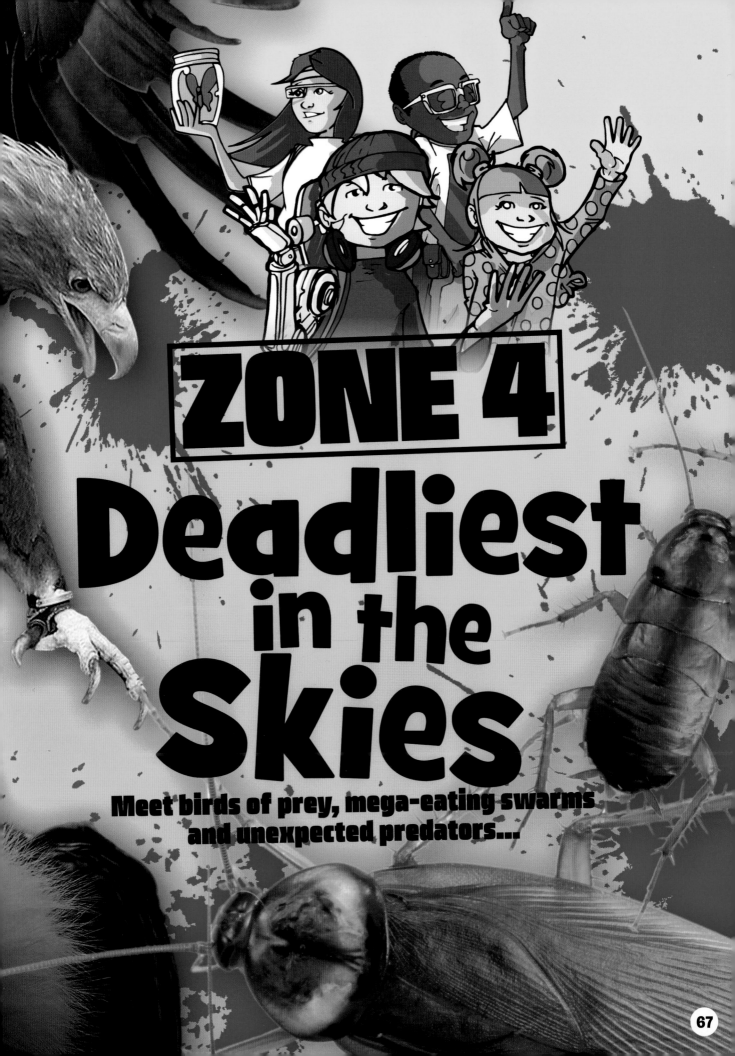

ZONE 4

Deadliest in the Skies

Meet birds of prey, mega-eating swarms and unexpected predators...

ZONE 4: Deadliest in the skies

the **lowdown**...

KILLER FACT

In 2013, a woman who fell to her death in the French Pyrenees was then eaten by Griffon Vultures.

Griffon Vulture

With its 2.8 m (9.2 ft) wingspan, this beastly looking bird doesn't hunt for food. It has a much more gruesome eating habit. It's a carnivorous raptor, a scavenger that seeks out dead, rotting flesh to feast upon. Yuk!

Scariest Carnivorous Birds

Some birds look like cute and fluffy feathered friends, but others look ready to tear their prey to pieces!

BIRD

1	**Griffon Vulture**
2	African Crowned Eagle
3	Marabou Stork
4	Vulturine Guineafowl
5	Turkey Vulture
6	California Condor
7	Shoebill
8	Harpy Eagle
9	Great Grey Shrike
10	Antarctic Giant Petrel

AFRICAN CROWNED EAGLE

Don't mess with this extremely large and powerful bird. It can weigh up to 4.5 kg (10 lb), with a wingspan of over 1.8 m (6 ft). This bird of prey has a big appetite and likes to hunt MONKEYS!

TEAM T-10 REPORT

Clean Freak

The Marabou Stork may snack on disgusting carrion (dead animals), but it's surprisingly picky about the cleanliness of its food. A Marabou Stork will sometimes wash food in water to remove dirt and soil before it eats it!

TOP 10 Fastest Airborne Predators

How fast do you think you can run? It's probably around 8 km/h (5 mph). So don't challenge the fastest bird on this list to a race - it's almost 78 times faster than you!

	TYPE	MAXIMUM KNOWN SPEED (KM/H)	(MPH)
1	Peregrine Falcon	389	241.7
2	Golden Eagle	320	198.8
3	Gyrfalcon	209	129.9
4	Swift	171	106.3
5	Eurasian Hobby	161	100
6	Frigate Bird	153	95.1
7	Spur-Winged Goose	142	88.2
8	Red-Breasted Merganser	130	80.8
9	Canvasback	116	72.1
10	Eider	113	70.2

GYRFALCON

The biggest bird of prey in our Top 10, this speedy raptor has a wingspan of up to 64 in (162.6 cm)! The Gyrfalcon is the official bird of Canada's Northwest Territories and has a long history of helping humans hunt.

Swift

Swift by name and swift by nature, these birds travel HUGE distances: up to 200,000 km (124,274 miles) in a year! There are about 100 different known species across the globe.

THE FRIGATE BIRD HAS A WINGSPAN OF 2.3 M (7.5 FT). IT CAN'T SWIM OR EVEN WALK VERY WELL, BUT SEE HOW FAST IT IS IN THE AIR!

KILLER FACT

If you're a fussy eater, the Golden Eagle puts you to shame... It hunts over 400 different animals for its dinner. Although it does eat reptiles, the Golden Eagle much prefers mammals' blood.

NOT JUST TOP OF THIS LIST, THE PEREGRINE FALCON IS ALSO THE FASTEST ANIMAL IN THE WORLD. ROUGHLY THE SIZE OF A CROW, FEMALES ARE MUCH BIGGER THAN THE MALES.

the lowdown...

Golden Eagle

Getting its name from those shimmering golden feathers, this bird is one of the most iconic animals on the planet. It is the most common national animal, with five nations picking it. The Golden Eagle mostly hunts small ground mammals but this 6.8 kg (15 lb) heavyweight bird will happily take on cattle. Its wingspan can reach 2.5 m (8.4 ft)!

TOP 10 Biggest Eagles

Eagles are magnificent (and massive) birds of prey, so we decided to dedicate an entire section to them! Rated by size of wingspan, these are the largest species in the world today...

	TYPE	WINGSPAN (M)	(FT)
1	Wedge-Tailed Eagle	2.84	9.4
2	Himalayan Golden Eagle	2.81	9.22
3	Martial Eagle	2.6	8.53
4	White-Tailed Eagle	2.53	8.30
5	Steller's Sea Eagle	2.5	8.20
6	Bald Eagle	2.3	7.55
=	Verreaux's Eagle	2.3	7.55
8	Harpy Eagle	2.24	7.35
9	Philippine Eagle	2.20	7.22
10	Crowned Eagle	1.9	6.23

Bald Eagle

This famous species is the national animal of the USA. Some Native American tribes consider the Bald Eagle a sacred bird and a symbol of peace, connected to a higher spiritual realm.

SIZE 'EM UP

Here's a useful at-a-glance look at how the wingspans of these three big birds compare...

WEDGE-TAILED EAGLE
WINGSPAN: 2.84 m (9.4 ft)

BALD EAGLE
WINGSPAN: 2.3 m (7.55 ft)

CROWNED EAGLE
WINGSPAN: 1.9 m (6.23 ft)

the lowdown...

White-Tailed Eagle

This hefty 6.8 kg (15 lb) hunter lives for over 20 years. It likes to eat fish, but it will also eat other birds. When it's in scavenger mode, it's known to go claw-to-claw with other animals to claim a carcass or steal food when the opportunity arises.

FEATHERS
Feathers make flight possible and also help camouflage birds against predators. They also make fantastic insulation and keep eggs and baby birds warm.

SOME SCOTTISH FISHERMEN USED TO THINK SEEING A WHITE-TAILED EAGLE AT SEA WOULD MAGICALLY MAKE FISH FLOAT TO THE SURFACE!

KILLER FACT

The rainforest-loving Harpy Eagle has 12.7 cm (5 in) long claws... Which means they are about the same size as a Grizzly Bear's!

73

TOP 10 Deadliest Flying Insects

Don't be fooled by the size of these bugs. They may be small but they can still be a serious hazard to your health!

	INSECT	DEADLY ACT(S)
1	Mosquito	Spreads deadly diseases when it drinks our blood
2	Tsetse Fly	Carries "sleeping sickness," which can be fatal
3	American Cockroach	Infestations spread disease
4	Locust	Swarms eat and destroy crops
5	Termite	Eats through wood and can destroy homes
6	Asian Giant Hornet	Deadly sting. 40 people die in Japan each year
7	Africanized Honey Bee	Highly aggressive bee that attacks in a swarm
8	Yellow Jacket Wasp	Repeatedly stings victim if aggravated
9	Assassin Bug	Bites can be fatal! 10,000 people die each year
10	Flying Ant	Some grow as big as a Tarantula and have painful bites

SIZE 'EM UP

Here's how these big bugs compare:

AMERICAN COCKROACH
LENGTH: 4 cm (1.6 in)

MOSQUITO
LENGTH: 1.5 cm (0.59 in)

ASIAN GIANT HORNET
LENGTH: 2.7 cm (1.06 in)

TEAM T-10 REPORT

Sizable Swarm

The largest known locust swarm consisted of a mind-blowing 12.5 TRILLION insects! And with each locust able to eat the equivalent of their own body weight in food in a day, a swarm can quicky work its devastating way through crops.

74

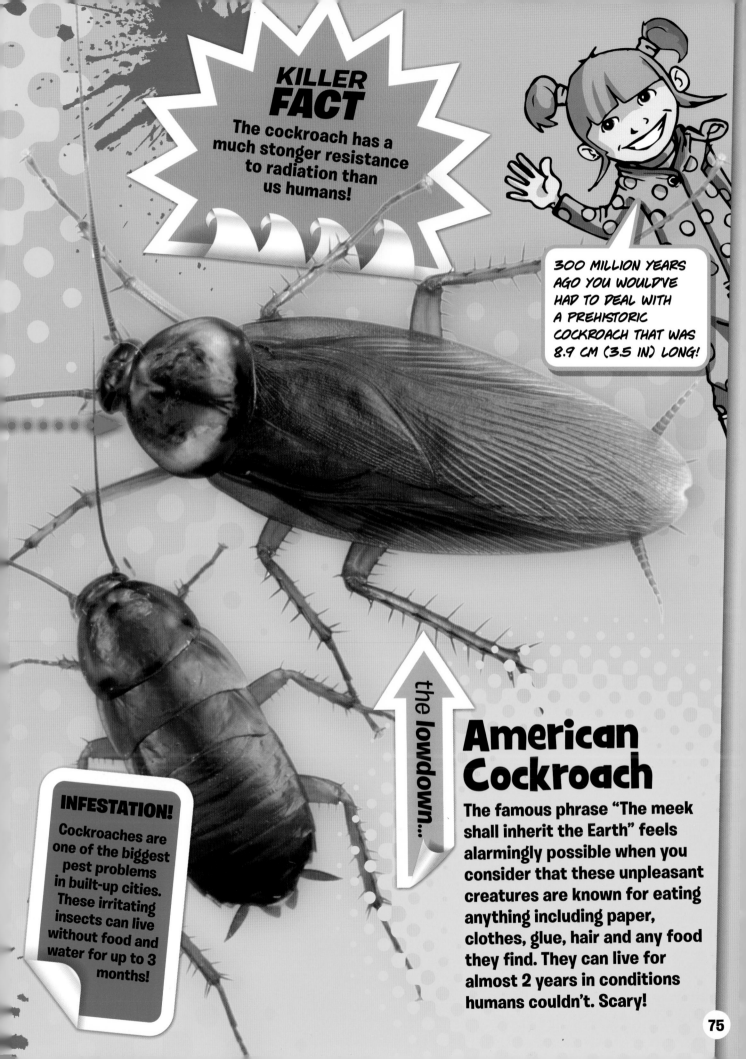

300 MILLION YEARS AGO YOU WOULD'VE HAD TO DEAL WITH A PREHISTORIC COCKROACH THAT WAS 8.9 CM (3.5 IN) LONG!

the lowdown...

American Cockroach

The famous phrase "The meek shall inherit the Earth" feels alarmingly possible when you consider that these unpleasant creatures are known for eating anything including paper, clothes, glue, hair and any food they find. They can live for almost 2 years in conditions humans couldn't. Scary!

INFESTATION!

Cockroaches are one of the biggest pest problems in built-up cities. These irritating insects can live without food and water for up to 3 months!

75

THE HERCULES BEETLE CAN LIFT MORE THAN 850 TIMES ITS OWN WEIGHT AND IT'S ONLY 17 CM (6.75 IN) LONG!

the lowdown...

Tarantula Hawk Wasp

If you're thinking, "This doesn't look like a spider," be prepared for a deadly fact that will astound you. This huge 5.1 cm (2 in) insect attacks and kills Tarantulas, dragging them to its nest for food for its larvae (babies)!

Flying Freaks

It's time to take to the skies and come face-to-face with some bizarre-looking animals that can fly or glide long distances.

	CREATURE
1	**Tarantula Hawk Wasp**
2	Devil Ray
3	Hercules Beetle
4	Pacific Flying Squid
5	California Condor
6	Holorusia brobdignagius Crane Fly
7	Draco Lizard
8	Flying Lemur
9	Large Flying Fox
10	Giant Petrel

KILLER FACT
Devil Rays leap high out of the water and glide with their wings. But nobody knows why!

FLYING LEMUR
There are only two kinds of this animal – the Philippine and the Sunda Flying Lemur – but both are actually a type of Colugo (a tree-dwelling mammal). They can glide for over 100 m (328 ft)!

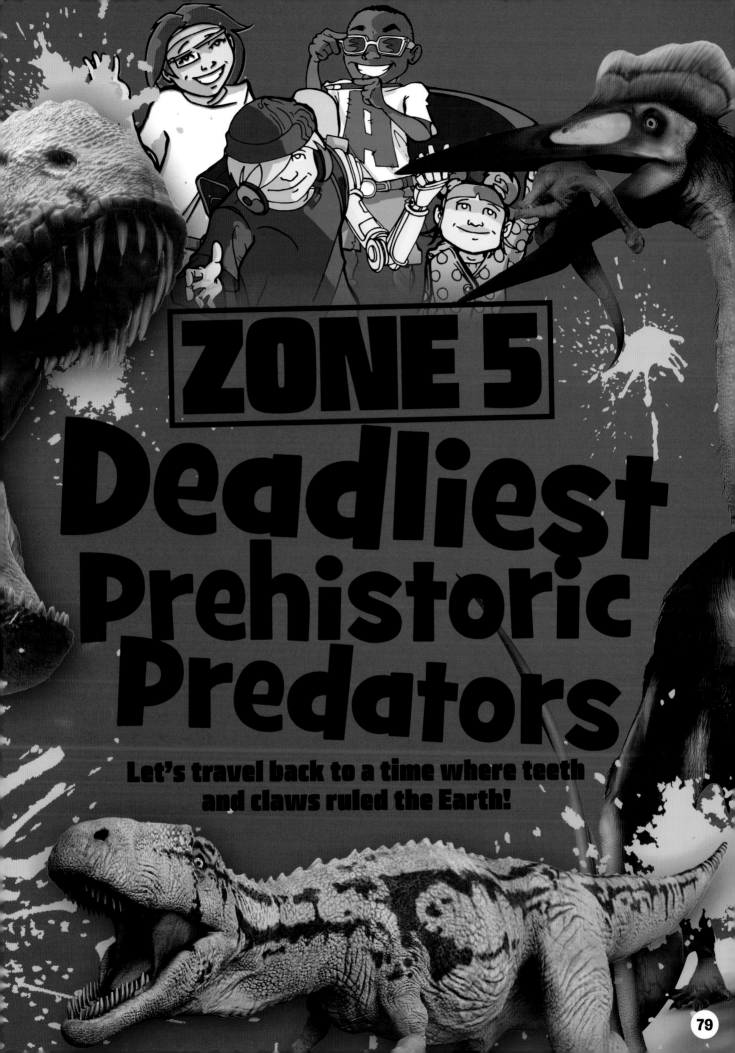

ZONE 5

Deadliest Prehistoric Predators

Let's travel back to a time where teeth and claws ruled the Earth!

TOP 10 Biggest Carnivorous Dinosaurs

Of all the meat-eating dinos that ruled the prehistoric era, these are the 10 titans that would have cast the biggest shadow.

KILLER FACT

So far, experts have unearthed and discovered more than 1,000 species of dinosaur!

the lowdown...

Carcharodontosaurus

The Carcharodontosaurus lived about 100 million years ago, and gets its long name because of its teeth. They look very similar to those of a Great White Shark, which has the Latin name of *Carcharodon carcharias*.

	TYPE	LENGTH (M)	(FT)
1	Spinosaurus	18	59
2	Carcharodontosaurus	13.2	43.3
=	Giganotosaurus	13.2	43.3
4	Chilantaisaurus	13	42.7
5	Tyrannosaurus rex	12.3	40.4
6	Tyrannotitan	12.2	40
7	Torvosaurus	12	39.4
=	Allosaurus	12	39.4
9	Acrocanthosaurus	11.5	37.7
10	Deltadromeus	11	36.1

SIZE 'EM UP

It's a battle of the heights...
T. rex vs. Spinosaurus vs. human!

SCIENTISTS BELIEVE THAT SOME OF THESE MASSIVE BEASTS COULD RUN AT UP TO 32.3 KM/H (20 MPH)!

"BIG AL" ALLOSAURUS

Back in 1991, a near-complete Allosaurus skeleton was discovered in the mountainous state of Wyoming. A group of experts led by team captain Kirby Siber excavated the fossilized bones of a dino they fondly named Big Al. It turned out they were only missing 5 percent of the entire Allosaurus skeleton!

TOP 10 Widest Prehistoric Wingspans

To put these measurements into perspective, the wingspan of a Boeing F-15 fighter jet is 13.05 m (42.10 ft)... the same as the biggest reptile in our Top 10!

SOME PTEROSAURS HAD TEETH, BUT THE POPULAR PTERANODON JUST HAD A BEAK AS PART OF ITS 2 M (6 FT) LONG HEAD.

	TYPE	WINGSPAN (M)	(FT)
1	Hatzegopteryx	13	42.7
2	Arambourgiania	11	36.1
3	Quetzalcoatlus	9	29.5
4	Pteranodon	8	26.2
5	Coloborhynchus	7	23
=	Moganopterus	7	23
7	Tupuxuara	6	19.7
=	Ornithocheirus	6	19.7
9	Cearadactylus	5.5	18
10	Thalassodromeus	4.5	14.8

HATZEGOPTERYX

This massive winged reptile was only discovered in 2002! A French paleontologist first found Hatzegopteryx remains in Transylvania, Romania, home of another frightening flying creature – Bram Stoker's fictional bloodsucker, Dracula.

SIZE 'EM UP

So many wingspans, so many measurements! Here's how these beasts would look next to a human...

HATZEGOPTERYX

PTERANODON

ORNITHOCHEIRUS

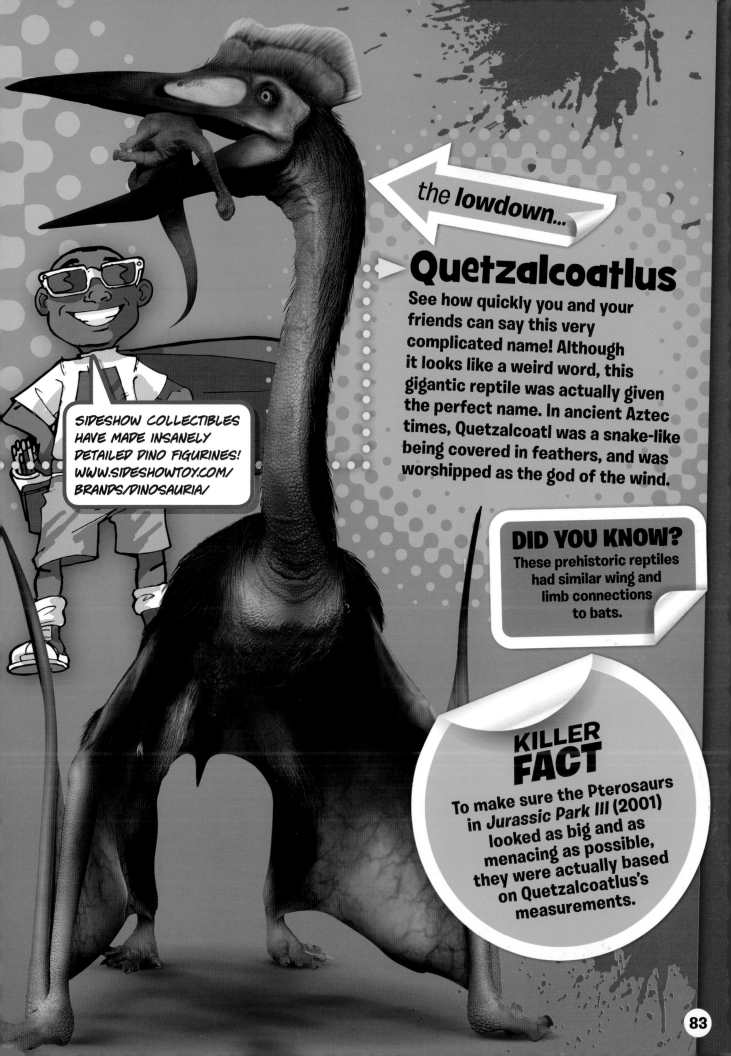

Quetzalcoatlus

See how quickly you and your friends can say this very complicated name! Although it looks like a weird word, this gigantic reptile was actually given the perfect name. In ancient Aztec times, Quetzalcoatl was a snake-like being covered in feathers, and was worshipped as the god of the wind.

SIDESHOW COLLECTIBLES HAVE MADE INSANELY DETAILED DINO FIGURINES! WWW.SIDESHOWTOY.COM/ BRANDS/DINOSAURIA/

DID YOU KNOW?
These prehistoric reptiles had similar wing and limb connections to bats.

KILLER FACT

To make sure the Pterosaurs in *Jurassic Park III* (2001) looked as big and as menacing as possible, they were actually based on Quetzalcoatlus's measurements.

TOP 10 Largest Ocean Beasts

If you thought that the Saltwater Crocodile and Whale Shark were big water beasts, check out the size of these aquatic prehistoric predators.

	CREATURE	TYPE	LENGTH (M)	(FT)
1	Mauisaurus	Reptile	20.1	66
2	Megalodon	Fish	20	65.6
3	Liopleurodon	Reptile	18	59
4	Leedsichthys	Fish	16	52.5
5	Mosasaurus	Reptile	15.2	49.9
=	Hainosaurus	Reptile	15.2	49.9
7	Elasmosaurus	Reptile	14	46
8	Pliosaurus	Reptile	12.2	40
=	Megalneusaurus	Reptile	12.2	40
=	Plotosaurus	Reptile	12.2	40

TEAM T-10 REPORT

Eyewitness!

What's the biggest aquatic reptile you've ever seen? And what about the largest fish? Carry out an investigation with your friends and compare the sizes of the underwater animals that you've seen with your own eyes.

SIZE 'EM UP

The Great White Shark is big enough at 7.9 m (26 ft), but the Megalodon was MASSIVE...

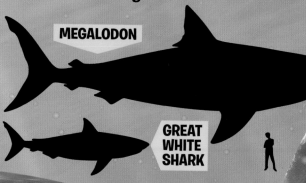

MEGALODON

GREAT WHITE SHARK

MEGALODON

This king of all sharks had very similar-shaped teeth to the Great White Shark. At 18 cm (7.1 in) long, Megalodon's were more than three times the length of a Great White's 5 cm (2 in) gnashers! Fossils of Megalodon teeth can fetch more than $600 in online auctions.

MEGALODON TOOTH

the lowdown...

Liopleurodon

Scientists have calculated that this ocean giant may have weighed 25 tons (55,116 lb)! Its huge flippers would have given it excellent swimming skills, but not necessarily speed. It would have been one of the top predators in our oceans 165 million years ago.

KILLER FACT

The first Mosasaurus skull was discovered in the Netherlands in 1764.

the **lowdown**...

Smilodon

This ancient big cat roamed North and South America over 2.5 million years ago. Smilodon's fangs were an impressive 27.9 cm (11 in) long and grew at an unbelievable rate of 7 mm (0.3 in) a month! Despite their size, the fangs were quite fragile.

KILLER FACT

As you can see by the size comparison to the average adult human, *Arctotherium angustidens* was a huge ancient bear that lived 1.2 million years ago. It makes the Polar Bear at 1,002 kg (2,209 lb) look like a big teddy bear!

SMILODON

ARCTOTHERIUM ANGUSTIDENS

TOP 10 Biggest Prehistoric Carnivorous Mammals

Dinosaurs weren't the only creatures hunting for their dinner in the prehistoric era. Some amazing mammals also stalked their prey, too.

THE MODERN-DAY TIGER HAS 10 CM (3.9 IN) CANINES, SO SMILODON'S WERE NEARLY THREE TIMES LONGER!

	CREATURE	WEIGHT (KG)	WEIGHT (LB)
1	Arctotherium angustidens	1,749	3,855.9
2	Pseudocyon	773	1,704.2
3	Smilodon	470	1,036.2
=	Ngangdong Tiger	470	1,036.2
5	Pachycrocuta	200	440.9
6	Dire Wolf	79	174.2
7	Epicyon	68	150
8	Megalictis ferox	60	132.3
9	Viverra leakeyi	41	90.4
10	Ekorus ekakeran	40	88.2

DIRE WOLF

The Dire Wolf was not, as many people might believe, a prehistoric giant. It was actually pretty much the same size as a modern Grey Wolf, but was a bulkier 79.4 kg (175 lb). Almost 1.2 million years ago, it roamed in packs searching for food.

TOP 10 Weirdest Prehistoric Creatures

You may have recognized some of the prehistoric beasts in this zone, but we bet that you've never heard of THESE weirdos.

KILLER FACT

If you think we've discovered all the dinosaurs and prehistoric creatures there were, think again. Scientists are unearthing roughly 15 new species every year!

CREATURE

1 Opabinia

2 Dunkleosteus

3 Desmatosuchus

4 Longisquama

5 Nothosaurus

6 Stethacanthus

7 Epidexipteryx

8 Deinotherium

9 Helicoprion

10 Sauroctonus

Epidexipteryx

We've looked at a lot of seriously massive prehistoric beasts in this zone, but this one was VERY small — just 25.4 cm (10 in) long! This tiny weirdo was hopping around 160 million years ago, and had simian and bird-like features. Fly, monkey-bird, fly!

the lowdown...

Nothosaurus

This 3 m (13 ft) prehistoric creature lurked in the water some 240 million years ago. Notosaurus was semi-aquatic, with webbed toes and terrifying long jaws lined with rows of extra-sharp, needle-like teeth. It hunted shoals of small fish, snapping them up with surprising speed.

GRAB SOME PAPER AND PENS AND COME UP WITH YOUR VERY OWN MADE-UP, SUPER-WEIRD DINOSAUR!

OPABINIA
LENGTH: 10 cm
(3.9 in)

TOP 10 Most Terrifying Dino Weaponry

This was a tough one, simply because so many dinosaurs had invincible scales and huge claws! Here are our fave 10 weaponized titans.

DID YOU KNOW?
The name *Tyrannosaurus rex* means "king of the tyrant lizards."

the **lowdown**...

T. rex

Possibly the most famous of all the dinosaurs, *Tyrannosaurus rex* has been very successfully excavated. Over 50 near-complete skeletons have been dug up since the first fossil was unearthed in 1902 by American Barnum Brown. The biggest *T. rex* teeth ever found were 30 cm (12 in) long!

TRICERATOPS'S NAME COULDN'T BE MORE ACCURATE. IT MEANS "THREE-HORNED FACE."

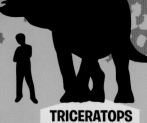

TRICERATOPS

	Dinosaur	Weaponry
1	**Spinosaurus**	Huge sail-like spines on its back and massive jaws
2	Phorusrhacidae	Terrifying 3 m (10 ft) tall bird with a big hooked beak
3	Triceratops	Strong 1 m (3 ft) long upper horns and imposing bulk
4	Liopleurodon	Powerful jaws that were 3 m (10 ft) long
5	Megalania	Komodo Dragon-like, but 7 m (23 ft) long
6	Therizinosauridae	Sickle-shaped claws on long-reaching arms
7	Tyrannosaurus rex	Curved, dagger-like teeth of multiple lengths
8	Megaraptor	Nearly 30 cm (12 in) long single front claws
9	Deinocheirus	Three very long hooked claws on each hand
10	Carcharontosaurus	Teeth just like a Great White Shark in a land lizard's body

MEGARAPTOR

PHORUSRHACIDAE WAS CALLED THE "TERROR BIRD" BUT IT COULDN'T ACTUALLY FLY! ITS BEAK COULD BE UP TO 46 CM (18 IN) LONG.

KILLER FACT
The 7.6 m (25 ft) long Megaraptor was a scary sight. Behind those deadly 30 cm (11.8 in) sickle-shaped claws was 2 tons (4,000 lb) of mass.

SPINOSAURUS

This beast could have weighed 21 tons (46,000 lb) and the distinctive spines on its back were 1.65 m (5.4 ft) long! The first ever Spinosaurus remains were excavated in 1912 but were tragically destroyed during Second World War bombings.

TIME TO GET INTERACTIVE!

That's it – our walk on the wild side with some seriously deadly animals is over. Wrap things up by putting your new knowledge to the test...

Questions from... ZONE 1

1 Which animal out of these three kills the most humans per year?

A B C

2 See if you know whether these facts about Polar Bears are true or false.

A: They weigh more than a Saltwater Croc.

TRUE   FALSE

B: Their Latin name means "sea bear."

TRUE   FALSE

C: Polar Bears can detect food nearly 1.6 km (1 mile) away.

TRUE   FALSE

3 Can you list these animals from 1-6 in order of the size of the pack they hunt in?

A: Wolf
B: Army Ant
C: Dolphin
D: Killer Whale
E: Piranha
F: Hyena

Questions from... ZONE 2

2 A The Huntsman and Hercules are types of what animal?

B What is the largest big cat, weighing in at 420 kg (925.9 lb)?

1 Can you identify these three deadly land animals just from seeing their silhouettes?

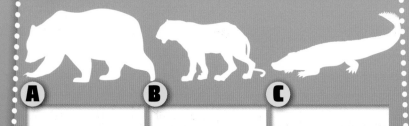

A   B   C

3 See if you can name this scary land predator from what you can see in this picture.

Questions from... ZONE 3

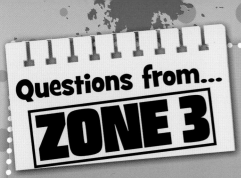

1 Can you name the only shark that appears in both the Top 10 Biggest Sharks and Top 10 Fastest Aquatic Predators lists?

2 See if you can name these two ocean-dwelling creatures.

A

B

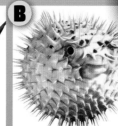

3 Check the place that's had the most shark attacks – a staggering 1,055 in total!

A: Europe

B: Australia

C: USA

Questions from... ZONE 4

1 Which predatory bird is the fastest in the skies, clocking a jaw-dropping 389 km/h (241.7 mph)?

2 Can you name this scary-looking carnivorous bird?

3 Can you name this creepy pest from this jumbled image?

Questions from... ZONE 5

1 Can you name this prehistoric big cat?

2 Which dinosaur was a whopping 12.3 m (40.4 ft) in length and had teeth measuring up to 30 cm (12 in) long?

A: *Tyrannosaurus rex* ...

B: Megaraptor ....

C: Spinosaurus ....

D: Triceratops ....

3 How long was Mauisaurus, the largest prehistoric creature in the ocean?

A: 18 m (59 ft)

B: 20.1 m (66 ft)

C: 14 m (46 ft)

D: 12.2 m (40 ft)

ANSWERS:

ZONE 5
1: Smilodon
2: A - *Tyrannosaurus rex*
3: B - 20.1 m (66 ft)

ZONE 4
1: Peregrine Falcon
2: Griffon Vulture
3: Cockroach

ZONE 3
1: Great White Shark
2: A - Sailfish, B - Pufferfish
3: C - USA

ZONE 2
1: A - Kodiak Brown Bear, B - Tiger,
C - Saltwater Crocodile
2: A - Spider, B - Tiger
3: Komodo Dragon

ZONE 1
1: A - Indian Cobra
2: A - FALSE, B - TRUE, C - TRUE
3: B, E, F, C, A, D.

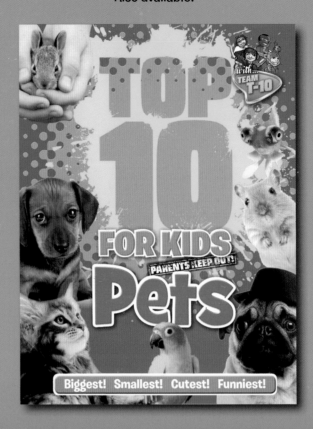
PICTURE CREDITS

All images supplied by © **Getty Images**

• •

ACKNOWLEDGMENTS

Top 10 Parents Keep Out! Pets Produced by SHUBROOK BROS. CREATIVE

Writer & Researcher: Paul Terry

Illustrations: Huw J

Chief Sub-editor: Claire Bilsland

• •

Special thanks to...

Ian Turp & Marc Glanville at Getty Images

David Martill, Palaeobiologist

Box office information courtesy of The Internet Movie Database (http://www.imdb.com).
Used with permission.

• •